for:

from:

date:

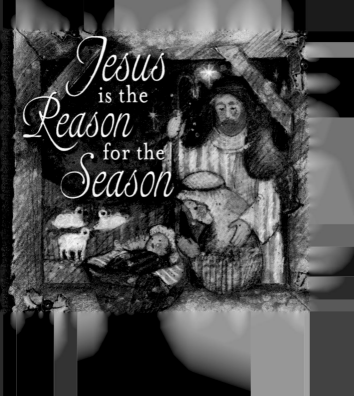

Little Treasures Miniature Books

Good Tidings of Great Joy

The Visit

The Christian faith is founded upon a well attested sober fact of history; that quietly, but with deliberate purpose, God himself has visited this little planet.

J.B. PHILLIPS

SWEET MAJESTY

Sometimes in the night it comes to me
That God, enthroned in awesome majesty,
Reveals in tend'rest, sweet simplicity
His love for man.

Did He, compassionate, know from the start
That I could take a baby to my heart;
That from a manger bed He could impart
His perfect plan?

And did He know, with shepherds in the night
My soul could take exultant, winged flight
And follow, joyously, a radiant light
To Bethlehem?

Here, as I kneel, with heart too full for speech,
I ponder how an angel choir could reach
Throughout all time, to all the world to teach
Peace! Peace to men!

MARION LIEN

The Christmas Story

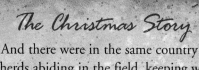

And there were in the same country
shepherds abiding in the field, keeping watch
over their flock by night. And, lo, the angel
of the Lord came upon them, and the *glory*
of the Lord shone round about them
and they were sore afraid.

And the angel said unto them,
"Fear not: for, behold, I bring you
good tidings of *great joy,* which
shall be to all people. For unto
you is born this day in the

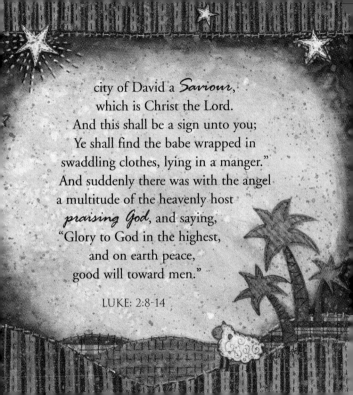

city of David a *Saviour*,
which is Christ the Lord.
And this shall be a sign unto you;
Ye shall find the babe wrapped in
swaddling clothes, lying in a manger."
And suddenly there was with the angel
a multitude of the heavenly host
praising God, and saying,
"Glory to God in the highest,
and on earth peace,
good will toward men."

LUKE: 2:8-14

It is good to be children sometimes, and never better than at Christmas, when its mighty Founder was a child himself.

CHARLES DICKENS

The only real blind person at Christmastime is he who has not Christmas in his heart.

HELEN KELLER

OLD CHRISTMAS CAROL

God rest you merry,
Gentlemen,

Let nothing you dismay;

Remember Christ
our Saviour,

Was born on
Christmas Day.

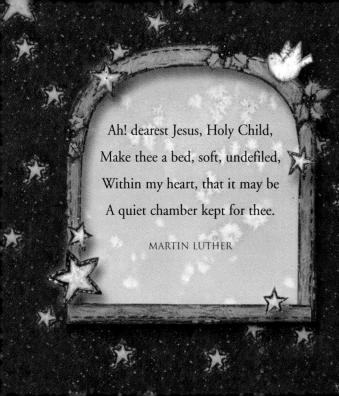

Ah! dearest Jesus, Holy Child,
Make thee a bed, soft, undefiled,
Within my heart, that it may be
A quiet chamber kept for thee.

MARTIN LUTHER

Christmas

Christmas is when
God came down the
stairs of heaven with a
baby in His arms.

Immanuel

Therefore the Lord himself will
give you a sign: The virgin will
be with child and will give birth
to a son, and will call him
Immanuel.

ISAIAH 7:14

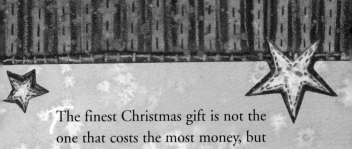

The finest Christmas gift is not the one that costs the most money, but the one that carries the most love.

HENRY VAN DYKE

What a terrific moment in history that was, when men first saw their God in the likeness of the weakest, mildest and most defenseless of all living creatures!

MALCOLM MUGGERIDGE

O Little Town of Bethlehem

O little town of Bethlehem,
How still we see thee lie!
Above thy deep and dreamless sleep
The silent stars go by.

PHILLIPS BROOKS

Good Tidings of Great Joy

Our Hearts His Bethlehem

Far, far away is Bethlehem,
And years are long and dim,
Since Mary held the Holy Child
And angels sang for Him.
But still to hearts where love and faith
Make room for Christ in them,
He comes again, the child from God,
To find His Bethlehem.

W. RUSSELL BOWIE

Good Tidings of Great Joy

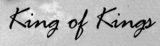

King of Kings

Not to those in soft apparel,
Was the savior first made known;
Not to noble or to high-born,
Or to courtiers round a throne;
Not to kings or mighty monarchs,
Was the King of Kings revealed,
But to poor and lonely shepherds
In the lonely pasture fields.

19TH CENTURY CHRISTMAS CARD

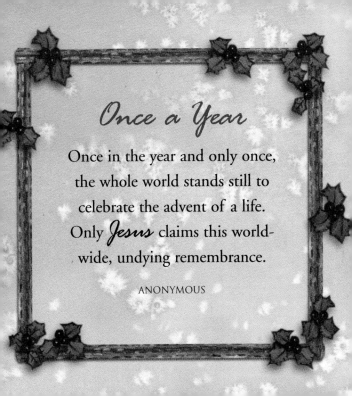

Once a Year

Once in the year and only once,
the whole world stands still to
celebrate the advent of a life.
Only *Jesus* claims this world-
wide, undying remembrance.

ANONYMOUS

Love Set Forth

Of course God might have chosen other methods. He might have sent forth His son trailing clouds of glory from the opened heavens with a legion of angels for His bodyguard. Or He might have revealed His presence by one of those strange and startling theophanies which are occasionally recorded in the Old Testament. He might have heralded His coming with earthquake, tempest, or the voice of thunder. But no! A Baby is born of a humble girl in the outhouse of a crowded inn; and Love has set forth on His mighty mission.

EDWARD GIBBON

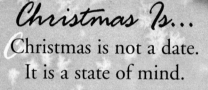

Christmas Is...

Christmas is not a date.
It is a state of mind.

MARY ELLEN CHASE

Christmas is the day that
holds all time together.

ALEXANDER SMITH

Christmas is based on
an exchange of *gifts*;
the gift of God to man –
his Son;
and the gift of man
to God – when we first
give ourselves to God.

VANCE HAVNER

We know how
God would
act if he were
in our place –
he has been
in our place.

A. W. TOZER

Jesus' coming is the final and unanswerable proof that God cares.

WILLIAM BARCLAY

Christmas began in the heart of God. It is complete only when it reaches the heart of man.

ANONYMOUS

And They Worshiped Him

The magi went on their way, and the star they had
seen in the east went ahead of them until it stopped
over the place where the child was. When they saw
the star, they were overjoyed. On coming to the
house, they saw the child with his mother Mary, and
they bowed down and worshiped him. Then they
opened their treasures and presented him with
gifts of gold and of incense and of myrrh.

MATTHEW 2:9-11

He clothed himself
with our lowliness
in order to
invest us with
His
grandeur.

RICHARDSON WRIGHT

A CHILD IS BORN

For to us a child is born, to us a son
is given, and the government
will be on his shoulders.

And he will be called
Wonderful Counselor, Mighty God,
Everlasting Father, Prince of Peace.

ISAIAH 9:6

THE SAVIOR

She will give birth to a
son, and you are to give
him the name Jesus,
because he will save his
people from their sins.

MATTHEW 1:21

Good Tidings of Great Joy

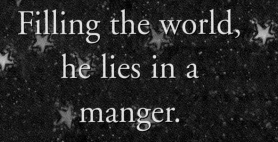

Filling the world,
he lies in a
manger.

SAINT AUGUSTINE

Jesus, my Savior

A Little Child

The shepherds had an angel
The wise men had a star;
But what have I,
a little child,
To guide me home from far
Where glad stars
sing together,
And singing angels are?

CHRISTINA ROSSETTI

A Bethlehem Manger

The coming of Christ by way of a Bethlehem manger seems strange and stunning. But when we take him out of the manger and invite him into our hearts, then the meaning unfolds and the strangeness vanishes.

C. NEIL STRAIT

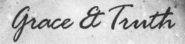

Grace & Truth

The Word became flesh
and made his dwelling
among us. We have seen his
glory, the glory of the
One and Only,
who came
from the Father,
full of grace and truth.

JOHN 1:14

Your Birthday

O Holy Infant, small and dear,
Your birthday once again is here,
And joyful songs ring near and far
Wherever little children are.

ANONYMOUS

*J*oy to the world, the Lord is come.
Let earth receive her King.

ISAAC WATTS

December 25

December 25 had been a Greek
festival day to the sun god.
In 386 A.D., John Chrysostom, the
eloquent preacher, first encouraged
Christians to celebrate December 25
as the birth of Jesus, the True Son,
instead. Within a hundred
years, the custom had become
widespread among Christians.

Starry, Starry Night

The stars were brighter than
    ever before.

The night was different,
    crackling with new beginnings.

Something was happening
    in the dark, smelly stable;

Gift of God was before us.

ANONYMOUS

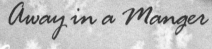

Away in a Manger

Away in a manger, no crib for a bed,
The little Lord Jesus laid down His
sweet head. The stars in the sky
looked down where He lay,
The little Lord Jesus,
asleep on the hay.

MARTIN LUTHER

Christmas is Eternal

Like God, Christmas is timeless
and Eternal, from everlasting
to everlasting. There was Christmas
in the heart of God before the world
was formed. He gave Jesus to us, the night the
angels sang, yes – but the Bible tells us that
Jesus shared a great glory with the Father
long before the world was made.
Jesus was always, too!

DALE EVANS ROGERS

Highest & Holiest

His life is the highest
and the holiest
entering in at
the lowliest door.

OSWALD CHAMBERS

A Christmas Prayer

Let not our hearts be busy inns,
That have no room for Thee,
But cradles for the living Christ
And His nativity.

RALPH S. CUSHMAN

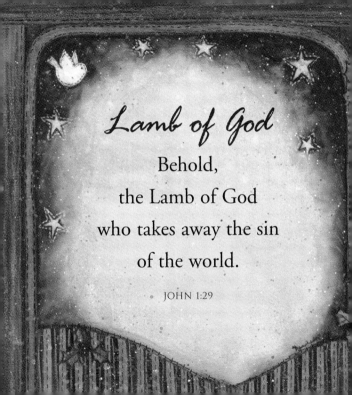

Lamb of God

Behold,

the Lamb of God

who takes away the sin

of the world.

JOHN 1:29

While continuing to be the
true God, he was born in a stable
and lived as a working man
and died on a cross.
He came to show us how to live,
not for a few years but
eternally.

FULTON OURSLER

HE SHOWED US
How TO LIVE

God, who had fashioned time and space in a clockwork of billions of suns and stars and moons, in the form of his beloved Son became a human being like ourselves. On the microscopic midge of planet he remained for thirty-three years. He became a real man, and the only perfect one.